Fact Finders®

WHAT YOU NEED TO KNOW ABOUT

MENINGITIS

BY RENEE GRAY-WILBURN

CONSULTANT:
MARJORIE J. HOGAN, MD
UNIVERSITY OF MINNESOTA
AND HENNEPIN COUNTY MEDICAL CENTER
ASSOCIATE PROFESSOR OF PEDIATRICS
AND PEDIATRICIAN

CAPSTONE PRESS
a capstone imprint

Fact Finders Books are published by Capstone Press,
1710 Roe Crest Drive, North Mankato, Minnesota 56003
www.capstonepub.com

Library of Congress Cataloging-in-Publication Data
Cataloging-in-Publication data is on file with the Library of Congress.
ISBN 978-1-4914-4832-8 (library binding)
ISBN 978-1-4914-4900-4 (paperback)
ISBN 978-1-4914-4918-9 (eBook PDF)

Developed and Produced by Focus Strategic Communications, Inc.
  Adrianna Edwards: project manager
  Ron Edwards: editor
  Rob Scanlan: designer and compositor
  Mary Rose MacLachlan: media researcher
  Francine Geraci: copy editor and proofreader
  Wendy Scavuzzo: fact checker

Capstone thanks the National Meningitis Association for their contributions to this book.
The information on pages 4–5, 14, and 21 are true stories used with permission from NMA.

Photo Credits
Alamy: David Hoffman Photo Library, 14, Mediscan, 29, Nucleus Medical Art Inc, 17, Radius Images, 15; Centers for Disease Control and Prevention, 25; Glow Images: Corbis/Jose Luis Pelaez, 26; iStockphoto: PicturePartners, 27, Shantell, 12; Library of Congress, 7; Science Source: Alfred Pasieka, 22, BSIP, 28, Evan Oto, 4, Jim Dowdalls, 10, Reed Business Publishing/Andrew Bezear, 11, Royal Victoria Infirmary, Newcastle upon Tyne/Simon Fraser, 5, SPL, cover (bottom); Shutterstock: A and N Photography, 13, Canit, 23 (bottom), Dziewul, 18, everything possible (background), back cover and throughout, GeorgeMPhotography, cover (top), 1 (top), hxdbzxy, 24, Ilike, 16, Sebastian Kaulitzki, 1 (bottom) and throughout, 8, 20, tab62, 19; SuperStock: Exactostock/George Doyle, 23 (top); U.S. National Library of Medicine, 6

Printed in China
042015   008831LEOF15

TABLE OF CONTENTS

CHAPTER 1
WHAT IS MENINGITIS?

"It feels like a bomb going off in my head!" That is how 15-year-old Brett described the pain to his doctor. The doctor examined Brett. Then he told him he had a disease called meningitis. Meningitis is an infection of the **meninges**. These tissues swell when they are infected. Brett had pain in his head and neck. This was caused by the swollen meninges squeezing against his brain and spinal cord.

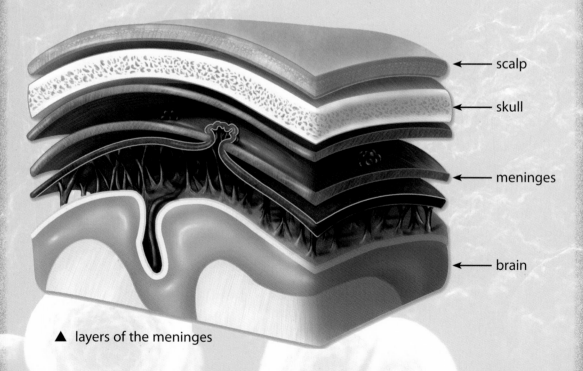

scalp

skull

meninges

brain

▲ layers of the meninges

meninges—three layers of tissue that surround the brain and spinal cord

Brett's brain tissue swelled so much that his body could not work properly. He could not get out of bed, eat solid food, or see very well. After many days of tests and treatment, Brett finally started to get better. He spent 15 days in the hospital. Then he spent another month resting at home. This helped Brett to recover.

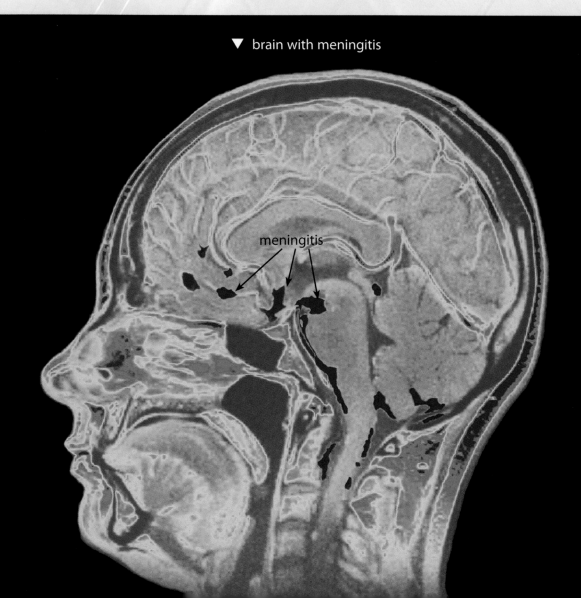

▼ brain with meningitis

meningitis

HISTORY OF MENINGITIS

The first record of meningitis was in 1805. That was the year an **outbreak** of meningitis happened in Switzerland. The next year the disease showed up in the United States for the first time.

Meningitis was once called brain fever. No one knew what caused this disease. Then, in 1887, Anton Weichselbaum, an Austrian scientist, made a discovery. He found that a type of **bacteria** could cause meningitis.

▲ Anton Weichselbaum

About 20 years later, American scientist Simon Flexner made a medicine from the blood of horses. This medicine kept many people from dying of meningitis. In the mid-1940s doctors used a new **antibiotic** called penicillin to treat meningitis. Forms of penicillin are still used today in treating the disease.

▼ Simon Flexner

TIMELINE OF MENINGITIS

1805	first medical record of meningitis by Swiss doctor Gaspard Vieusseux
1806	first case reported in United States
1887	Anton Weichselbaum discovers bacteria that causes meningitis
1891	Doctor Heinrich Quincke uses first spinal tap to test spinal fluid for meningitis bacteria
1905	major meningitis epidemic in Africa, killing thousands of people
1905–07	U.S. scientist Simon Flexner develops a medicine from horses to kill meningitis bacteria
1928	Alexander Fleming discovers penicillin, the world's first antibiotic
1944	first successful use of penicillin in treating meningitis
1974	first vaccine for meningitis is approved
1996–2007	more than 20,000 die from meningitis outbreak in Africa
2005–10	additional vaccines are licensed to protect against four of five major meningitis-causing bacteria

▶ Alexander Fleming

outbreak—when a number of people get sick at the same time from the same germ source

bacteria—one-celled, microscopic living things that exist all around you and inside you; many bacteria are useful, but some cause disease

antibiotic—a drug that kills bacteria and is used to cure infections and disease

TYPES OF MENINGITIS

There are five main types of meningitis: viral, bacterial, fungal, parasitic, and **noninfectious**. Meningitis that is caused by a **fungus** or a **parasite** cannot be spread from person to person. The same is true of noninfectious meningitis. Only meningitis caused by a **virus** or bacteria can spread from person to person.

VIRAL MENINGITIS

Viral meningitis is the most common type. This is a serious illness, but it is not usually deadly. It is caused by viruses spread through sneezing, coughing, saliva, or unwashed hands after going to the bathroom.

Having the virus does not mean that you will get meningitis. Meningitis happens only when the virus infects the meninges cells. Children under 5 years old and others with weak **immune systems** have the greatest chance of getting viral meningitis.

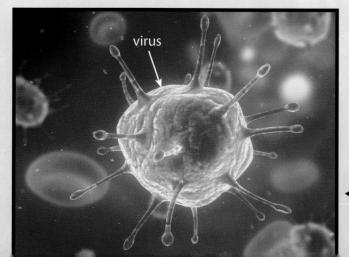

virus

◀ virus

Can Meningitis Spread from Person to Person?

Viral ——▶ Yes
Bacterial ——▶ Yes
Fungal ——▶ No
Parasitic ——▶ No
Noninfectious ——▶ No

MENINGITIS

Type	Cause	How Do You Get It?
Viral	Virus that infects the meninges	A meningitis-causing virus can enter the body through an infected person's sneeze or cough.
Bacterial	Bacteria that infect the meninges	By having very close contact with an infected person for an extended period of time, such as being at camp together or sharing a room
Fungal	Fungus that spreads from a person's bloodstream into the spinal cord	By taking certain medicines that weaken the immune system or by inhaling fungal spores of bird droppings found in the soil
Parasitic	A parasite found in warm bodies of fresh water, such as lakes and rivers, swimming pools, etc.	A parasite can enter through a person's nose and travel up into the brain.
Noninfectious	Head injuries, certain medications, some cancers, and brain surgery	Many other causes, besides infection, can result in swelling of the meninges.

noninfectious—an illness or disease not caused by germs

fungus—a single-celled organism that lives by breaking down and absorbing the natural material it lives in

parasite—an animal or plant that lives on or inside another animal or plant and causes harm

virus—a germ that infects living things and causes diseases

immune system—the part of the body that protects against germs and diseases

BACTERIAL MENINGITIS

Bacterial meningitis is rare. But it is the most dangerous kind of meningitis. Its **symptoms** come on suddenly. The disease may cause serious problems. It can even cause death if it is not treated in time. Bacterial meningitis is a type that can cause outbreaks.

symptom—a sign that suggests a person is sick or has a health problem

▼ Bacteria attack the meninges tissues.

Just like viruses that cause meningitis, bacteria can spread from person to person. Healthy people can have meningitis-causing bacteria in their noses or throats without getting sick. These people are called carriers. But if a person's immune system is weak, it may not be able to fight off the bacteria. If bacteria reach the meninges, then meningitis could result.

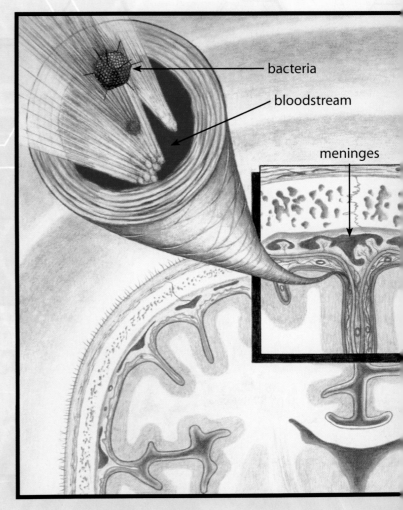

bacteria

bloodstream

meninges

▶ Meningitis-causing bacteria travel from an infection in the body, through the bloodstream, and to the meninges.

HEALTH FACTS

- In the early 1900s, 75 to 80 percent of people who had meningitis died.
- From 2003 to 2007, there were about 4,100 cases and 500 deaths each year from the disease in the United States.
- By 2013 there were fewer than 1,000 cases per year in the United States, with 100 to 150 deaths.
- About 20 percent of people who get bacterial meningitis are between 11 and 24 years old.

CHAPTER 2

SYMPTOMS OF MENINGITIS

Have you ever had the flu? If so, you probably remember having a fever, headache, sore muscles, and maybe nausea. Meningitis patients can have these same symptoms. But there are big differences between the flu and meningitis. Both illnesses can cause headaches. But most people with meningitis describe that headache as the worst they ever had.

▲ If you have aches and a fever, staying in bed is a good idea.

Meningitis can make light hurt the eyes. It can also cause rashes or bruises.

A person with meningitis may have only some of these symptoms. And the symptoms of bacterial and viral meningitis look and feel the same. The only way to diagnose the disease is through lab tests.

HEALTH FACT

The flu can make you feel achy all over. But with meningitis, you will usually feel severe pain in the neck and sometimes in the back.

▼ lab testing for meningitis

NICHOLAS' STORY

One day when Nicholas was 8 years old, he felt very sick. He had a bad headache, stomach pain, and started coughing a lot. Sometimes he vomited when he coughed. His mom took him to the hospital. They sent him home, saying it was just the flu. But overnight, Nicholas got much worse. The tiniest bit of light hurt his eyes. And the lightest touch or breeze on his legs caused pain all the way up his back. It felt like someone was stabbing him with a sword.

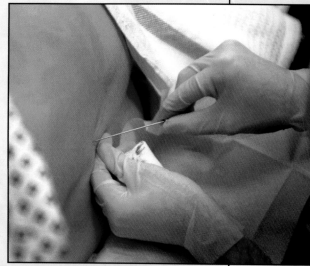

He went back to the hospital. The doctors put a long needle in his spine to pull out fluid. The fluid was supposed to be clear. But Nicholas' was so cloudy it was almost a solid color. The doctors said he had bacterial meningitis. They started giving him medicine through a tube in his arm to kill the infection.

▲ testing for meningitis by pulling out fluid from the spine

Nicholas was in the hospital for a week. After he went home, it took another week until he was able to walk on his own again. This happened over 10 years ago. But Nicholas still gets pain in his back because of the meningitis.

HOW ARE THEY DIFFERENT?

Disease	Symptoms
Flu	Fever/chills, cough, sore throat, runny or stuffy nose, muscle or body aches, headache, feeling tired, vomiting
Viral meningitis	High fever, severe headache, stiff neck, **seizures**, sensitivity to bright light, sleepiness or trouble waking up, nausea/vomiting, lack of appetite, lack of energy
Bacterial meningitis	Fever and chills, changes in behavior (such as confusion), severe headache, stiff neck, seizures, sensitivity to bright light, sleepiness or trouble waking up, nausea/vomiting, small red marks on the skin (severe cases)

▶ Some symptoms of the flu are similar to symptoms of meningitis.

seizure —sudden attack of illness caused by brain swelling or other symptoms; also called a convulsion

TESTING FOR MENINGITIS

If you have symptoms of meningitis, a doctor will order laboratory tests to confirm the diagnosis. The tests may include a CT, or CAT, scan. This is a special X-ray that creates 3-D pictures of the body or its organs. Doctors will also take samples of your blood, urine, and spinal fluid. They may also take a saliva sample from your throat to check for any meningitis-causing bacteria.

These tests show what kind of meningitis a person has. They can also identify the type of virus or bacteria causing it. This is important information to help doctors decide how to treat it.

▼ taking a saliva sample to test for meningitis

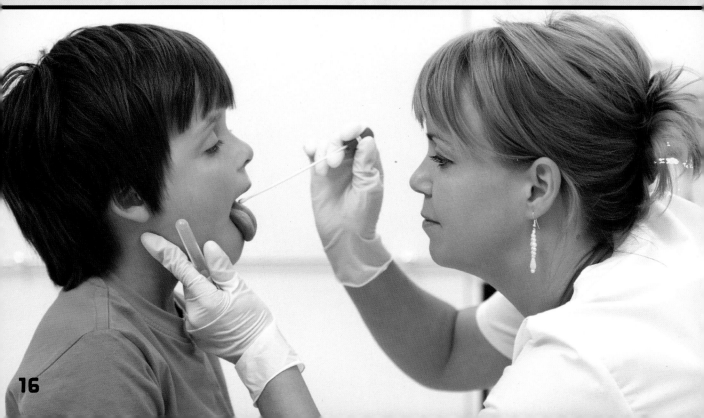

SPINAL TAP

To test for meningitis, doctors take fluid from the spine. This is called a spinal tap. First they numb the area near the bottom of the backbone using a pain-killing drug. Then they insert a long needle into the spinal cord. They withdraw some spinal fluid. Healthy fluid is clear. Fluid containing meningitis bacteria is cloudy.

▼ how a spinal tap works

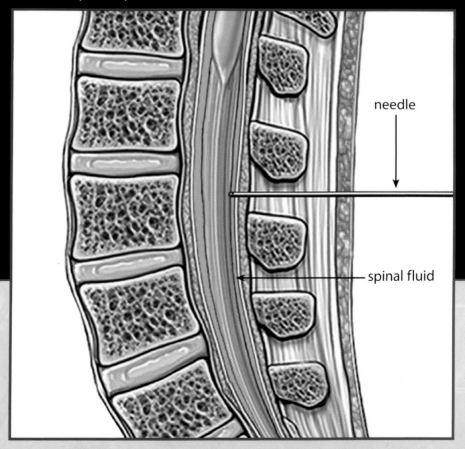

needle

spinal fluid

CHAPTER 3

HOW IS IT TREATED?

Test results show what type of meningitis a person has. But doctors give the patient antibiotics right away, before the results come in. This helps stop any possible bacterial infections. A tube with a needle is placed into a vein in the hand, arm, or chest. That way the drugs can go directly into the patient's bloodstream.

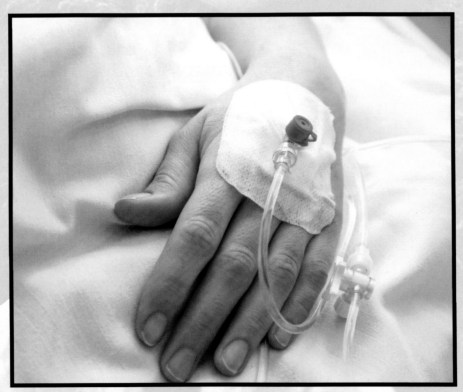

▲ Drugs enter the bloodstream through a tube and needle.

VIRAL MENINGITIS

If the tests show viral meningitis, antibiotics are stopped because they do not work on viruses. Medicine that attacks specific viruses may be given instead.

Most patients with viral meningitis get better on their own in one or two weeks. They may not even need to stay in a hospital. Most just need plenty of rest, fluids, and medicine for pain. They can recover fully, with no lasting problems. Other people may continue to have headaches, tiredness, and memory loss from viral meningitis.

▼ It is important to drink a lot of water to recover from meningitis.

BACTERIAL MENINGITIS

People with bacterial meningitis usually stay in the hospital for a week or longer. They continue to receive antibiotics while doctors watch for other symptoms. These can include swelling in the brain, **shock**, and seizures.

Bacterial meningitis has many possible after-effects. Some are not as serious, such as headaches, sore muscles, weakness, and poor appetite. Other effects can last a long time and even be dangerous. About 15 percent of patients will end up with brain damage, organ damage, memory loss, speech problems, or loss of vision or hearing.

▶ A swollen brain is one of the symptoms of meningitis.

shock—a medical condition caused by a dangerous drop in blood pressure and flow; people suffering from shock can die

If bacteria show up in the test samples, the lab begins to grow them. It takes a few days to grow enough bacteria to study. But this is an important step. It helps doctors know what kind of bacteria they have to treat.

MIKE'S STORY

Mike went to the hospital with bacterial meningitis. His fever reached 105.9° F (41°C). He fell into a coma. When Mike finally woke up, he could not hear. He also could not walk or lift his arms or legs. He had to be fed through a tube in his stomach.

Finally Mike was able to leave the hospital. But then he needed to do special exercises to help him to sit up, stand, and walk again. After several months Mike was able to walk using a cane. In time he was able to walk without any help. During this time he also got implants for his ears to help him hear again.

Mike also suffers from mental after-effects of meningitis. His short-term memory is poor. He has a hard time making decisions. Mike is depressed about how meningitis still affects him. But he tries to have a good attitude. He tries his best every day.

AFTER-EFFECTS OF BACTERIAL MENINGITIS

Meningitis bacteria cause the meninges to swell. The swollen tissues put pressure on the brain. This causes brain damage. It can last a short time or go on for years. It may change a person's memory, mood, and behavior. The bacteria can also damage the body's organs. This can cause many problems.

Bacteria that cause meningitis can get into a person's bloodstream. They multiply in the blood and release poisons that can destroy blood vessels. They can reduce the amount of oxygen that flows throughout the body. Without enough oxygen, the person's organs and limbs may start to die. Some people need to have damaged tissue replaced. Others may lose arms or legs because of blood poisoning.

▼ meningitis bacteria

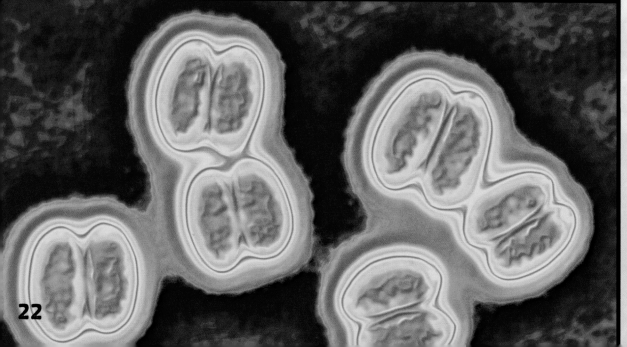

SOME POSSIBLE AFTER-EFFECTS FROM BACTERIAL MENINGITIS

- balance problems
- cerebral palsy
- behavioral changes
- blindness or vision loss (temporary or permanent)
- clumsiness
- concentration problems
- deafness or hearing loss
- depression
- tiredness
- emotional changes
- epilepsy
- headaches
- sore joints or stiffness
- learning difficulties
- memory problems
- mood swings
- temper tantrums
- ringing in ears

▲ blindness

 ▶ headaches

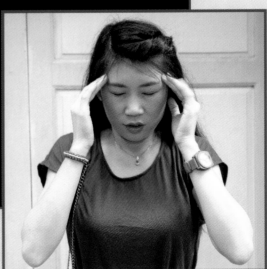

CHAPTER 4

PREVENTING MENINGITIS

Anyone can get bacterial meningitis. But three things can affect your risk—your age, your lifestyle, and where you live.

Infants are the most at risk for this disease. That is because their immune systems are not strong enough to fight off the disease. Teens and young adults are also a high-risk group. That is because the disease spreads easily in crowded places, such as schools.

People who live or work closely together are at greater risk. This includes young people in the military and college students living on campus. People who travel to countries where there is an outbreak are at risk. Health care workers who care for meningitis patients are also at risk.

▼ college students on campus

THE MENINGITIS BELT

Developing countries are at greater risk. That is because they are often overcrowded and have unsafe water and poor health care. The highest-risk area is the Meningitis Belt in Africa. It spreads across several African countries below the Sahara Desert. The belt stretches from Senegal in the west (on the Atlantic Ocean) to Ethiopia in the east (on the Indian Ocean).

Outbreaks usually occur during Africa's dry season, from December through June. During these months the area is very dry and dusty. Many people get colds and other infections that weaken their immune systems. This increases the chances of getting meningitis.

During an outbreak one in every 1,000 people can get the disease. The largest outbreak ever recorded in Africa was in 1996–97. More than 20,000 people died. By comparison the United States has fewer than 1,000 cases every year in the entire country.

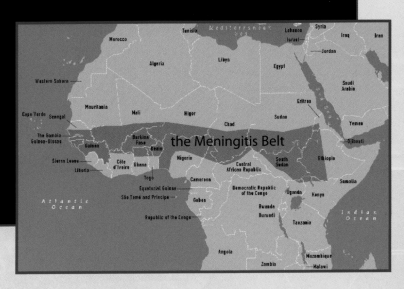

the Meningitis Belt

VACCINES

The good news is there are things you can do to lower your chances of getting meningitis. The best way is to get vaccinated. This means getting a shot that helps protect you from the disease. No vaccine will protect you completely. But vaccines help your body build up a defense.

▼ Vaccines help to protect against meningitis.

HEALTHY LIFESTYLE

Keeping clean is important in helping to prevent any disease. Always wash your hands before eating and after using the toilet. Regular hand-washing will help keep you healthy.

Having a strong immune system also helps fight off disease. You can do this by eating healthy foods, exercising, and getting enough sleep.

HEALTH FACT

Keep your immune system healthy. Kids over age 6 need three to four servings of fruits and vegetables, one hour of exercise, and 10 to 11 hours of sleep every day.

▼ Washing hands regularly helps prevent catching disease.

QUICK ACTION

Meningitis requires quick action. If you think you have caught the disease, tell your parents or a trusted adult and see a doctor right away. Antibiotics may help protect you. But you must take them as soon as possible.

▼ A doctor examines a child for meningitis.

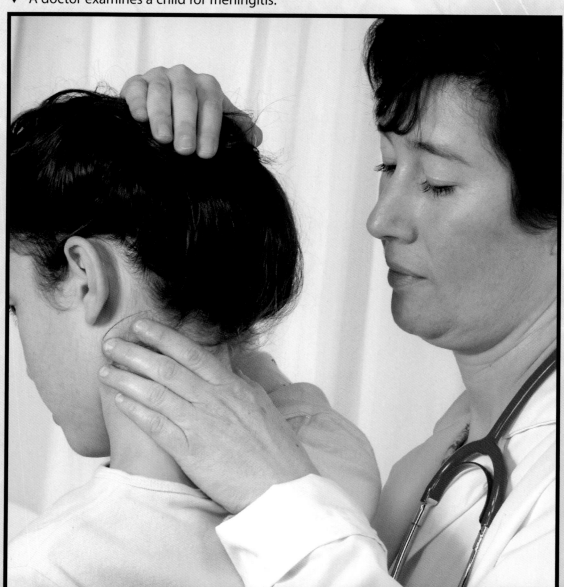

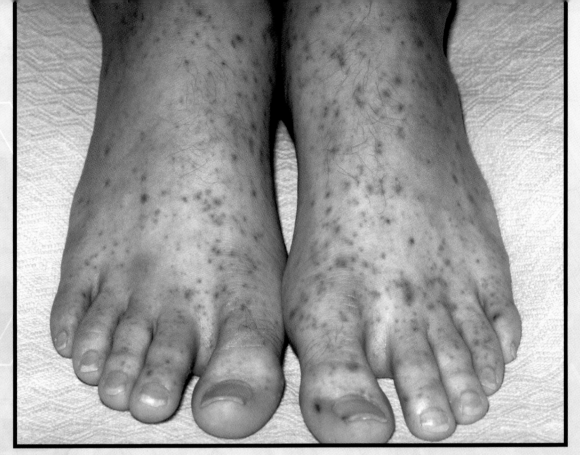
▲ meningitis body rash

Knowing what symptoms to look for could save your life. Some of the symptoms include severe headache, neck pain, fever, nausea, sleepiness, and body rash. If you have most or even some of these symptoms, see a doctor right away.

People who live in countries with access to good health care may have less chance of getting the disease. Vaccines and other medicines help people to stay healthy. But learning about this disease—and knowing what to do about it—is the best defense.

GLOSSARY

antibiotic (an-ti-bye-OT-ik)—a drug that kills bacteria and is used to cure infections and disease

bacteria (bak-TEER-ee-uh)—one-celled, microscopic living things that exist all around you and inside you; many bacteria are useful, but some cause disease

fungus (FUHN-guhs)—a single-celled organism that lives by breaking down and absorbing the natural material it lives in

immune system (i-MYOON SISS-tuhm)—the part of the body that protects against germs and diseases

meninges (men-IN-jeez)—three layers of tissue that surround the brain and spinal cord

noninfectious (NON-in-FEKT-shus)—an illness or disease not caused by germs

outbreak (OWT-brayk)—when a number of people get sick at the same time from the same germ source

parasite (PAIR-uh-site)—an animal or plant that lives on or inside another animal or plant and causes harm

seizure (SEE-zhur)—a sudden attack of illness caused by brain swelling or other symptoms; also called a convulsion

shock (SHOK)—a medical condition caused by a dangerous drop in blood pressure and flow; people suffering from shock can die

symptom (SIMP-tuhm)—a sign that suggests a person is sick or has a health problem

virus (VYE-ruhss)—a germ that infects living things and causes diseases

READ MORE

Abramovitz, Melissa. *Meningitis*. Diseases and Disorders. Farmington Hills, Mich.: Lucent Books, 2015.

Goldsmith, Connie. *Meningitis*. Twenty-First Century Medical Library. Minneapolis: Twenty-First Century Books, 2008.

Klosterman, Lorrie. *Meningitis*. Health Alert. New York: Marshall Cavendish Benchmark, 2007.

Kneib, Martha. *Meningitis*. Epidemics! Deadly Diseases Throughout History. New York: Rosen Publishing Group, 2005.

Willett, Edward. *Meningitis*. Diseases and People. Springfield, N.J.: Enslow Publishers, 1999.

INTERNET SITES

FactHound offers a safe, fun way to find Internet sites related to this book. All of the sites on FactHound have been researched by our staff.

Here's all you do:

Visit *www.facthound.com*

Type in this code: 9781491448328

 Check out projects, games and lots more at
www.capstonekids.com

INDEX